Wing Sauces

The Ultimate Recipe Guide

Copyright

Copyright © 2015 Encore Publishing. All rights reserved under International and Pan-American Copyright Conventions. No rights granted to reproduce this book or portions thereof in any form or manner whatsoever without the express written permission of the copyright owner(s).

Legal Notice

All content in this book is provided on an "As Is" basis. The authors and publishers provide no guarantees regarding the results of any advice or recommendations contained herein. Please note that much of this book is based on personal experiences of the author(s) and anecdotal evidence they have gathered. Although the author and publisher have made every reasonable attempt to achieve accuracy of the content of this book, they assume no responsibility for its veracity, or for any errors or omissions. Nothing in this book is intended to replace common sense, medical, legal or other professional advice; and this book is meant only to be informative and entertaining. Encore Books and its authors shall not be liable in the event of incidental or consequential damages in connection with, or arising out of, the providing of the information offered here.

Any trademarks, service marks, product names or named features are assumed to be the property of their respective owners, and are used herein for reference purposes only. There is no implied endorsement for any products or services mentioned in this publication.

Encore Book Club

Fabulous Free eBook Cookbooks Every Week!

We promote our eBooks FREE for the first 5 days of every publication. You will be the first to know when new books are published – as many as 5 books per week! That is a lot of books! Not to mention we frequently offer exclusive promotions. Our collection includes hundred's of books that encompasses a wide variety of topics including healthy natural foods, food allergy alternatives, gourmet meals, desserts, and easy and inexpensive meals. Just to name a few.

Sign-up at:

www.encorebookclub.com

View a complete list of our

Best Selling Recipe Book Series:

www.encorebookclub.com/booklist

Table of Contents

1) Stroganoff Wing Sauce
2) Chimichurri Wing Sauce
3) Mustard, Hot Pepper &Worcestershire Wing Sauce
4) Creamy Balsamic Vinegar Wing Sauce
5) Shallots & Red Wine Wing Sauce
6) Garlic, Butter & Herbs Wing Sauce
7) Chili Wing Sauce
8) Brandy, Parsnip & Cream Wing Sauce
9) Béarnaise Wing Sauce
10) Watercress, Hazelnut & Red Chili Wing Sauce
11) Black Bean Wing Sauce
12) Horseradish Wing Sauce
13) Balsamic Vinegar & Honey Wing Sauce
14) Peppercorn Wing Sauce
15) Sesame Wing Sauce
16) Japanese Wing Sauce
17) White Wing Sauce
18) Black Pepper Wing Sauce
19) Mayonnaise, Vinegar & Paprika Wing Sauce
20) Gorgonzola &Cream Wing Sauce
21) Mushroom & Cream Wing Sauce
22) Cranberry & Teriyaki Wing Sauce
23) Ranch & Salsa Wing Sauce
24) Red Miso Wing Sauce
25) Mushrooms, Chives & Miso Wing Sauce
26) Hollandaise Wing Sauce
27) Salsa Verde Wing Sauce
28) Garlic & Mayonnaise Wing Sauce
29) Butter, Rosemary & Balsamic Vinegar Wing Sauce
30) Jalapeno & Caramelized Onion Wing Sauce
31) Scallion Wing Sauce

1) Stroganoff Wing Sauce

Preparation Time: none
Cooking Time: 20 minutes
Ready In: 20 minutes
Servings: 2

INGREDIENTS:

1 cup beef stock
½ pound mushrooms, sliced
4 tablespoons soured cream
1 teaspoon plain flour
1 teaspoon tomato purée
1 small onion, chopped
1 garlic clove, chopped
1 teaspoon smoked paprika
2 tablespoons brandy
2 tablespoons butter
Small handful parsley, chopped
Salt and Pepper as per taste

DIRECTIONS:

1.
Place a large frying pan over medium-low heat and add half of the butter for melting.

2.
Once the butter melts, add the onions and cook for about 10 minutes or until the onions become soft.

3.
Now add the mushrooms and garlic and increase the heat. Cook till the liquid evaporates completely.

4.
Now add the paprika, flour and tomato puree to this mixture and cook for 1 minute.

5.

Pour in the brandy now and let the sauce bubble for 1 – 2 minutes. (Be careful while pouring the brandy as it may catch fire).

6.
Now pour the beef stock and increase the heat to reduce the sauce by half.

7.
Now blend the sour cream in the sauce and season with salt and pepper. Sprinkle the parsley. Serve warm!

2) Chimichurri Wing Sauce

Preparation Time: 5 minutes
Cooking Time: none
Ready In: 5 minutes
Servings: 2

INGREDIENTS:

2 teaspoons red wine vinegar
1 shallot, chopped
2 garlic cloves
Juice of 1/2 lemon
1/2 teaspoon oregano, fresh or dried
1/2 teaspoon chilli flakes
2 1/2 tablespoons olive oil
Small bunch parsley, roughly chopped
Salt and Pepper as per taste

DIRECTIONS:

1.
Chop the shallot, parsley, garlic, oregano and chili flakes very finely in a food processor or grinder.

2.
Now add 2 tablespoons olive oil, red wine vinegar, lemon juice and seasoning and blend / pulse to combine everything nicely. Spoon it over hot chicken wings and serve!

3) Mustard & Hot Pepper Wing Sauce

Preparation Time: 5 minutes
Cooking Time: none
Ready In: 5 minutes
Servings: 4

INGREDIENTS:

2 tablespoons prepared yellow mustard
4 drops hot pepper sauce (like Tabasco)
2 tablespoons Worcestershire sauce
1 1/4 cups ketchup
1 1/2 tablespoons apple cider vinegar
Salt and Pepper as per taste

DIRECTIONS:

1.
Mix the mustard, hot pepper sauce, Worcestershire sauce, ketchup and vinegar in a large bowl.

2.
Season with salt and pepper. Cook chicken wings in sauce or serve over already cooked wings.

4) Creamy Balsamic Vinegar Wing Sauce

Preparation Time: none
Cooking Time: 15 minutes
Ready In: 15 minutes
Servings: 4

INGREDIENTS:

½ pound button mushrooms, cleaned and quartered
2/3 cup dry sherry
1 tablespoon whole grain mustard
1/2 cup beef stock
2 tablespoons crème fraîche
1 garlic clove, lightly crushed
1 tablespoon balsamic vinegar
2 tablespoons chopped parsley
1 spring thyme
2 tablespoons olive oil

DIRECTIONS:

1.
Place a large pan over medium heat and add the olive oil to it. Once the oil is hot enough add the garlic, thyme and mushrooms and fry the mushrooms. Stir constantly.

2.
Now pour about 2/3 of the sherry in the pan and cook for 3 – 5 minutes to reduce the sherry to a glaze.

3.
Pour the vinegar and cook for a few seconds. Pour the remaining sherry and stock and bring the sauce to a boil. Reduce the flame and let the sauce simmer for 2 minutes.

4.
Now remove the garlic and thyme from the pan carefully and add the crème fraîche and mustard to the sauce.

5.
Season the sauce with salt and pepper. Serve warm over your chicken wings

5) Shallots & Red Wine Wing Sauce

Preparation Time: none
Cooking Time: 15 minutes
Ready In: 15 minutes
Servings: 2

INGREDIENTS:

3/4 cup red wine
1 large shallot, minced
2 to 3 tablespoons cold unsalted butter, cubed
Salt and pepper as per taste

DIRECTIONS:

1.
Reserve the drippings from cooking your chicken wings. Add the shallots to these drippings and cook over medium heat for about 2 minutes or until the shallots turn golden. (If you do not have the drippings, use olive oil for this).

2.
Now pour the red wine to the pan and stir using a wooden spoon. Scrape off any browned shallot bits and stir with the wine.

3.
Let the shallots and wine cook for about 7 minutes bringing the sauce to a boil. By this time the sauce will have reduced by half and become slightly syrupy.

4.
Now start adding the butter one cube at a time to the sauce to bring a glaze to the sauce.

5.
Season with salt and pepper and serve with your cooked chicken wings.

6) Garlic, Butter & Herbs Wing Sauce

Preparation Time: 5 minutes
Cooking Time: none
Ready In: 5 minutes
Servings: 6

INGREDIENTS:

1 bunch fresh chives, chopped
1 teaspoon dry rosemary
2 teaspoons garlic, minced
8 ounces unsalted butter, cubed and at room temperature
Salt and pepper as per taste

DIRECTIONS:

1.
Mix all ingredients in a large bowl and refrigerate for 1 hour.

2.
Spoon over on top of your cooked chicken wings (also over a nice steak.)

7) Chili Wing Sauce

Preparation Time: none
Cooking Time: 15 minutes
Ready In: 15 minutes
Servings: 4

INGREDIENTS:

1 teaspoon chilli sauce
1 tablespoon tomato sauce
1 tablespoon Worcestershire sauce
1 tablespoon barbeque sauce
1 tomato, chopped
1 large onion, chopped
1 teaspoon corn flour
2 teaspoons vinegar
2 tablespoons Olive Oil

DIRECTIONS:

1.
Place a medium sized frying pan over medium heat and add the olive oil to it. Once the oil is hot enough add the onions and tomato and cook until the onions become soft. This should take about 5 minutes.

2.
Now add the tomato sauce, Worcestershire sauce, chili sauce and barbeque sauce to the pan and stir carefully.

3.
Add the vinegar and bring the sauce to a boil. Reduce the flame and let the sauce simmer until it is reduced a little. About 5 minutes.

4.
Dissolve the corn flour in 2 tablespoons water and add to the sauce for thickening it a bit. Serve over hot chicken wings.

8) Brandy & Cream Wing Sauce

Preparation Time: 20 minutes
Cooking Time: 20 minutes
Ready In: 40 minutes
Servings: 4

INGREDIENTS:

2-3 tablespoons cognac or brandy
2 small-medium sized parsnips
1/2 cup cream, plus 1/4 cup extra
3/4 cup Chicken Stock
2 tablespoons butter
1 shallot, finely diced
2 brown mushrooms, sliced
1-2 teaspoons garlic, crushed
2 tablespoons Olive oil
Salt and white pepper as per taste

DIRECTIONS:

1.
Place a large deep saucepan over medium heat and pour the chicken stock and 1/2 cup cream in it. Let them get heated nicely. Reduce the heat if you start seeing bubbles.

2.
Meanwhile, peel the parsnips and remove their cores. Cut them into small dices.

3.
Add the cut parsnips to the cream and stock, season with salt and white pepper and let it simmer until it becomes completely soft.

4.
When done, strain the parsnips and reserve the cooking liquid. Now put the cooked parsnips in a food processor and pulse. Add the cooking liquid when needed to make a smooth puree.

5.

In a small frying pan over medium-low heat, melt the butter and add the mushrooms and shallots. Cook them until they turn golden.

6.
Now add the garlic and cook quickly. Remove from the heat and add the brandy. Return the pan to heat and let it cook for a few seconds.

7.
Now pour the remaining cream and cook until the sauce becomes thick. Serve as a dipping sauce with hot chicken wings.

9) Béarnaise Wing Sauce

Preparation Time: 10 minutes
Cooking Time: 5 minutes
Ready In: 15 minutes
Servings: 6

INGREDIENTS:

2 tablespoons minced shallots
1/4 cup good white wine
1/4 cup Champagne or white wine vinegar
3 tablespoon chopped fresh tarragon leaves, divided
3 extra-large egg yolks
1/2 pound unsalted butter, melted
2 tablespoons Olive Oil
Salt and ground black pepper as per taste

DIRECTIONS:

1.
Place a small saucepan over medium heat and add the Champagne vinegar, white wine, tarragon leaves, shallots, salt and pepper and stir.

2.
Bring the mixture to a boil and then let it simmer for about 5 minutes over medium heat or until the mixture reduces to a few tablespoons. Remove from heat and let it cool slightly.

3.
Put this mixture in a blender with the egg yolks and some salt and blend for 30 seconds.

4.
Now pour the hot melted butter in the blender and the remaining tarragon leaves and blend only for a few seconds. If the sauce is too thick, add a tablespoon of white wine to thin.

5.
Serve as a dipping sauce with hot chicken wings.

10) Watercress, Hazelnut & Red Chili Wing Sauce

Preparation Time: 10 minutes
Cooking Time: 15 minutes
Ready In: 15 minutes
Servings: 2

INGREDIENTS:

3 ounces watercress
1 red Chilli, deseeded and roughly sliced
4 ounces blanched hazelnuts
1 tablespoon balsamic vinegar, plus 2 teaspoons
1½ tablespoons olive oil, plus extra for griddling
Salt and pepper as per taste

DIRECTIONS:

1.
Preheat the oven to 350°F and place the hazelnuts on a baking tray. Toast them in the heated oven for 5 – 10 minutes until golden. Remove from the oven and let them cool a little.

2.
Put the toasted nuts, chili, watercress, olive oil and vinegar and seasoning in a food processor and pulse until they are finely chopped. The mixture should be a little coarse and not completely smooth.

3.
When your chicken wings are ready, spoon the mixture over the top. Sprinkle some watercress on top and serve!

11) Black Bean Wing Sauce

Preparation Time: 5 minutes
Cooking Time: 15 minutes
Ready In: 20 minutes
Servings: 2

INGREDIENTS:

1/4 cup fermented black beans
1 tablespoon all purpose flour
1 shallot, minced
1/2 cup dry white wine
1 cup whipping cream
1 tablespoon fresh lemon juice
1/2 cup unsalted butter, chilled, cut into 4 pieces
1 tablespoon butter (room temperature)
Salt and pepper as per taste

DIRECTIONS:

1.
In a small bowl add the room temperature butter and 1 tablespoon flour and mix to form a paste.

2.
In a separate medium sized saucepan boil the wine and shallots for about 3 minutes until the wine is slightly reduced.

3.
Now add the cream and black beans and increase the flame. Bring the sauce to a boil.

4.
Now add the flour paste and simmer until the sauce thickens. This should take about 1 minute. Reduce the heat to low.

5.
Now start adding the butter one piece at a time stirring until the butter melts. Let one piece melt completely before adding the next.

6.
Now pour the lemon juice and season with salt and pepper. Stir and after a few seconds remove the pan from the heat.

7.
Serve the sauce with your hot chicken wings.

12) Horseradish Wing Sauce

Preparation Time: 5 minutes
Cooking Time: none
Ready In: 5 minutes
Servings: 2

INGREDIENTS:

1 tablespoon fresh horseradish, grated
2 tablespoons good-quality natural yoghurt
1 lemon, juiced
1 tablespoons extra virgin olive oil
Salt and ground black pepper as per taste

DIRECTIONS:

1.
In a small bowl combine the yogurt and horseradish and season it with salt and pepper.

2.
Now squeeze the lemon juice in the bowl and add the olive oil to it and mix again.

3.
Use as a dipping sauce with hot chicken wings.

13) Balsamic Vinegar & Honey Wing Sauce

Preparation Time: none
Cooking Time: 15 minutes
Ready In: 15 minutes
Servings: 2

INGREDIENTS:

3/4 cup balsamic vinegar
1/4 cup honey
2 sliced shallots
2 tablespoons Worcestershire sauce
1 tablespoon mustard
2/3 cup ketchup
1/4 teaspoon allspice
1 teaspoon Sugar
1 teaspoon Butter
Salt and pepper as per taste

DIRECTIONS:

1.
Place a deep saucepan over medium heat and add the vinegar, honey, shallots, ketchup, Worcestershire sauce, mustard, sugar, allspice, salt and pepper in it and let everything simmer for about 15 minutes until the sauce thickens.

2.
Strain the sauce and then whisk in the butter. Use to cook with your chicken wings are as a separate sauce.

14) Peppercorn Wing Sauce

Preparation Time: 2 minutes
Cooking Time: 15 minutes
Ready In: 17 minutes
Servings: 4

INGREDIENTS:

2 to 3 tablespoons mixed peppercorns
1 shallot, minced
½ cup beef stock
¼ cup heavy cream
½ cup brandy
¼ cup butter
Salt to taste

DIRECTIONS:

1.
Crush the peppercorn using mortar and pestle or a rolling pin. Keep aside.

2.
Place a medium sized saucepan over medium-high heat and melt the butter in it.

3.
Add the shallots to the butter and cook until they become soft. This should take about 3 minutes.

4.
Now add the beef stock to the pan and bring to a boil. Let it boil for about 3 minutes.

5.
Now add the cream to this mixture and reduce the heat to medium. Let the sauce get heated nicely but don't let it boil.

6
When the sauce reaches your desired thickness add the salt. Serve over hot chicken wings.

15) Sesame Wing Sauce

Preparation Time: 5 minutes
Cooking Time: none
Ready In: 5 minutes
Servings: 4

INGREDIENTS:

1/4 cup Tahini (sesame seed paste)
1 tablespoon mayonnaise
2 tablespoons soy sauce
1 1/2 teaspoons ginger, ground
1 clove garlic, minced
1 pinch paprika
1/4 cup water

DIRECTIONS:

1.
In a medium sized bowl mix the mayonnaise, soy, tahini, minced garlic, ground ginger and paprika.

2.
Start stirring in the water until the desired consistency is reached. Serve as a dipping sauce with your chicken wings.

16) Japanese Wing Sauce

Preparation Time: 5 minutes
Cooking Time: none
Ready In: 5 minutes
Servings: 4

INGREDIENTS:

1/2 cup sesame seeds, toasted
1/2 cup onion, chopped
1 large garlic clove, minced
3/4 cup soy sauce
1 egg yolk
1/2 tablespoon dry mustard
1/2 cup whipping cream
1 cup vegetable oil

DIRECTIONS:

1.
In a food processor or blender, add the sesame seeds, onions, garlic and soy sauce and blend for 30 seconds.

2.
Now add the egg yolk, mustard, whipping cream and vegetable oil and blend again till everything becomes fine in consistency. Serve with hot chicken wings.

17) White Wing Sauce

Preparation Time: 3 minutes
Cooking Time: Refrigeration overnight
Ready In: 3 minutes (excluding the time for refrigeration)
Servings: 4

INGREDIENTS:
1 1/2 tablespoons white vinegar
1/2 teaspoon dry mustard powder
1-1/2 teaspoons tomato paste
1 tablespoon melted butter
1/2 teaspoon garlic powder
1/4 teaspoon paprika
2 teaspoon sugar
1 egg
1/4 cup water
3/4 cup soybean oil
Salt and cayenne pepper as per taste

DIRECTIONS:
1.
Put 1/4 cup oil, vinegar, mustard powder, egg, 1 teaspoon sugar, salt and pepper in a blender and blend everything for about 5 – 10 seconds.

2.
On low speed and start drizzling the remaining oil in it while it is running. Blend for about 30 seconds.

3.
Once done, take out the contents of the blender in a large mixing bowl. Add the remaining sugar, tomato paste, garlic powder, paprika and melted butter to this bowl and mix everything nicely.

4.
If the sauce is too thick add some water and stir until the desired consistency is achieved. Refrigerate the sauce overnight.

5.
Before serving, take out the sauce from the fridge and bring at room temperature.

18) Black Pepper Wing Sauce

Preparation Time: none
Cooking Time: 5 minutes
Ready In: 5 minutes
Servings: 2

INGREDIENTS:

½ cup red wine
2 tablespoons black peppercorn, pounded using mortar and pestle
½ cup beef broth
4 tablespoons heavy cream
1/2 teaspoon Worcestershire sauce
1/2 teaspoon cornstarch dissolved in 2 teaspoon water

DIRECTIONS:

1.
In a large saucepan over medium heat, add the red wine and let it simmer for a few seconds to allow it to reduce.

2.
Add the black peppercorn, beef broth, Worcestershire sauce and cream. Let this mixture simmer for a few seconds and then add the cornstarch solution to thicken the sauce.

3.
Spread the black pepper sauce over chicken wings and serve.

19) Mayonnaise, Vinegar & Paprika Wing Sauce

Preparation Time: 10 minutes
Cooking Time: 1 hour for refrigeration
Ready In: 1 hour 10 minutes
Servings: 6 – 8

INGREDIENTS:

3 tablespoons rice wine vinegar
1 cup mayonnaise
3 tablespoons chicken stock or water
3 tablespoons white granulated sugar
1 ½ teaspoons sweet paprika
1 ½ teaspoons garlic powder
2 tablespoons melted butter

DIRECTIONS:

1.
In a large mixing bowl whisk all the ingredients together until they are combined nicely.

2.
Refrigerate the sauce for an hour before serving with your chicken wings.

20) Gorgonzola & Cream Wing Sauce

Preparation Time: 10 minutes
Cooking Time: 1 hour
Ready In: 1 hour 10 minutes
Servings: 4

INGREDIENTS:

3 ounces gorgonzola cheese, crumbled
4 cups heavy cream
3 tablespoons parmesan cheese, grated
1/8 teaspoon ground nutmeg
Salt and pepper as per taste

DIRECTIONS:

1.
Place a large saucepan over medium heat and pour the heavy cream in it. Bring it to a boil. Then reduce the heat and let the cream simmer till it reduces by half, stirring occasionally. This should take about an hour.

2.
Remove the pan from the heat and add the cheeses, nutmeg, salt and pepper and stir until the cheese has completely melted.

3.
Serve as a dipping sauce.

21) Mushroom & Cream Wing Sauce

Preparation Time: none
Cooking Time: 15 minutes
Ready In: 15 minutes
Servings: 2

INGREDIENTS:

½ pound button mushrooms, cut in half then sliced
½ cup heavy cream
1 teaspoon olive oil
2 cloves of garlic, crushed
Salt and pepper as per taste

DIRECTIONS:

1.
Place a medium sized saucepan over medium-high heat and add the olive oil to it. Once the oil is hot enough add the mushrooms. Stir fry them until they turn golden brown and then reduce the heat to medium.

2.
Now add the cream to the mushrooms and season with salt and pepper. Let it cook for about 5 – 8 minutes, stirring occasionally but take care that the cream does not over boil.

3.
Once the sauce reduces to half its original quantity, add the crushed garlic and cook for 1 minute.

4.
Remove the sauce from the heat and serve with chicken wings.

22) Cranberry & Teriyaki Wing Sauce

Preparation Time: none
Cooking Time: 25 minutes
Ready In: 25 minutes
Servings: 2

INGREDIENTS:

1/2 cup dried cranberries, chopped
1/4 cup teriyaki sauce
1/2 cup good white wine
2/3 cup white onion, diced
1 teaspoon fresh garlic, minced
1/4 cup soy sauce
1/2 cup brown sugar
1/4 teaspoon cayenne pepper

DIRECTIONS:

1.
Place a medium sized saucepan over medium-high heat and add the Teriyaki sauce, white wine, soy sauce, onion, garlic, sugar and pepper. Cook until the mixture comes to a boil, stirring constantly.

2.
Once it starts boiling reduce the heat and let it simmer for about 5 minutes.

3.
Now add the cranberries and stir over low heat for 15 minutes. Remove from the heat and serve with hot chicken wings.

23) Ranch & Salsa Wing Sauce

Preparation Time: 5 minutes
Cooking Time: 1 hour (refrigeration)
Ready In: 1 hour and 5 minutes
Servings: 2

INGREDIENTS:

1 cup ranch style dressing
1/2 cup mild salsa
1 cup sour cream

DIRECTIONS:

1.
Mix all ingredients in a large bowl and refrigerate for an hour.

2.
Remove from fridge and serve with your cooked chicken wings.

24) Red Miso Wing Sauce

Preparation Time: 5 minutes
Cooking Time: none
Ready In: 5 minutes
Servings: 4 – 6

INGREDIENTS:

- 6 tablespoons red miso
- 2 tablespoons mirin
- 1 tablespoon tobanjan
- 5 medium garlic cloves, minced
- 2 tablespoons sake
- 2 tablespoons granulated sugar

DIRECTIONS:

1.
In a large bowl mix the miso, garlic, mirin, tobanjan, garlic, sake and sugar until everything is thoroughly combined.

2.
Serve as a sauce over hot chicken wings or you could even use this as a marinade while cooking.

25) Mushrooms, Chives & Miso Wing Sauce

Preparation Time: none
Cooking Time: 10 minutes
Ready In: 10 minutes
Servings: 4

INGREDIENTS:

½ pound mushrooms
1 tablespoon soy sauce
2 tablespoons chopped chives
1 1/2 tablespoons white miso paste
2 tablespoons heavy cream
1 cup quality chicken stock
1 tablespoon sunflower oil
1/2 teaspoon sugar

DIRECTIONS:

1.
In a medium sized deep saucepan heat the sunflower oil over medium-high heat.

2.
Add the mushrooms to this and cook them for 1 – 2 minutes or until they become soft.

3.
Now add the stock, cream, soy sauce, sugar and miso and bring the mixture to a boil. Stir occasionally.

4.
Once boiled, reduce the flamed and cook the sauce over low heat for 1 – 2 minutes until it thickens slightly.

5.
Serve with your cooked wings and chives at the side!

26) Hollandaise Wing Sauce

Preparation Time: 15 minutes
Cooking Time: 5 minutes
Ready In: 20 minutes
Servings: 2

INGREDIENTS:

8-10 fresh basil leaves, finely chopped
1/2 teaspoon white wine vinegar
2 large egg yolks
1 stick butter
Juice of 1 lemon
1 teaspoon cold water
Salt as per taste

DIRECTIONS:

1.
In a small pan add the egg yolks along with the salt, water and vinegar and whisk it for 1 – 2 minutes until it starts to thicken and turn pale.

2.
Slightly heat water in a pan larger than the pan containing the egg mix and put the egg pan over the water pan. Be careful that the bottom of the egg pan does not touch the water pan.

3.
Continue to whisk the eggs for about 3 minutes over the heating water pan or until they turn pale and thick. After this remove the egg pan.

4.
Melt butter in a small pan and mix it into the egg mixture. Keep stirring while mixing the butter until all the butter in completely mixed with the eggs and the sauce is thick and smooth.

5.
Season with salt and pepper and right before serving squeeze the lemon in the sauce and add the basil.

27) Salsa Verde Wing Sauce

Preparation Time: 15 minutes
Cooking Time: 5 minutes
Ready In: 20 minutes
Servings: 2

INGREDIENTS:

1 cup flat leaf parsley
2 anchovy filets
1 teaspoon red wine vinegar
1 garlic clove
1/3 cup extra virgin olive oil
Salt as per taste

DIRECTIONS:

1.
Put all the ingredients in a food processor and pulse until they turn into a smooth sauce.

2.
Serve as a dipping sauce with hot chicken wings.

28) Garlic & Mayonnaise Wing Sauce

Preparation Time: 5 minutes
Cooking Time: none
Ready In: 5 minutes
Servings: 2

INGREDIENTS:

1 garlic clove, crushed
4 tablespoons mayonnaise
Small handful chopped fresh tarragon

DIRECTIONS:

1.
In a small bowl put the mayonnaise and add the garlic and tarragon to it.

2.
Serve as a dipping sauce with hot chicken wings.

29) Butter, Rosemary & Balsamic Vinegar Wing Sauce

Preparation Time: 15 minutes
Cooking Time: 15 minutes
Ready In: 30 minutes
Servings: 4

INGREDIENTS:

8 tablespoons chilled unsalted butter, divided
2 large fresh rosemary sprigs
1/2 cup balsamic vinegar
1 large shallot, minced
2 tablespoons orange juice
Salt and pepper as per taste

DIRECTIONS:

1.
In a small heavy saucepan over medium heat melt 6 tablespoons of the butter.

2.
Add the shallots to the melted butter and cook till they become tender. This should take about 2 minutes.

3.
Add the rosemary and balsamic vinegar to this and simmer till the sauce has reduced to half cup. This should take about 6 minutes. Remove from heat when done. The sauce will separate, it is expected!

4.
After about 15 minutes, remove the rosemary sprigs from balsamic sauce and add orange juice to it. Bring the sauce to simmer over medium heat.

5.
Remove from heat and add the remaining 2 tablespoons butter. Whisk until the butter melts and gets fully incorporated in the sauce and the texture of the sauce becomes smooth.

30) Jalapeno & Caramelized Onion Wing Sauce

Preparation Time: none
Cooking Time: 25 minutes
Ready In: 25 minutes
Servings: 4

INGREDIENTS:

2 medium yellow onions, thinly sliced
2 fresh jalapeño peppers, thinly sliced
2 garlic cloves, thinly sliced
1/2 cup heavy cream
1 tablespoon Worcestershire sauce
2 teaspoons apple cider vinegar
2 teaspoons sugar
2 tablespoons unsalted butter
Salt and pepper as per taste

DIRECTIONS:

1.
Place a large skillet over medium heat and add the butter to it for melting.

2.
Once the butter melts add the onions, jalapenos, Worcestershire sauce, garlic, sugar, salt and pepper and cover the skillet. Let everything cook covered for about 15 – 20 minutes until the vegetables turn soft and golden. Stir occasionally.

3.
Now add the cream and stir. Cook for 2 minutes.

4.
Stir in the vinegar now and check the seasoning.

5.
Serve over hot chicken wings.

31) Scallion Wing Sauce

Preparation Time: 5 minutes
Cooking Time: none
Ready In: 5 minutes
Servings: 4

INGREDIENTS:

15 scallions, very thinly sliced
3 tablespoons vegetable oil
1/4 cup fish sauce
2 tablespoons toasted sesame seeds
2 tablespoons red wine vinegar

DIRECTIONS:

1.
Mix all ingredients in a large bowl.

2.
Serve as a marinade of dipping sauce with your cooked wings.

Encore Book Club

Fabulous Free eBook Cookbooks Every Week!

We promote our eBooks FREE for the first 5 days of every publication. You will be the first to know when new books are published – as many as 5 books per week! That is a lot of books! Not to mention we frequently offer exclusive promotions. Our collection includes hundred's of books that encompasses a wide variety of topics including healthy natural foods, food allergy alternatives, gourmet meals, desserts, and easy and inexpensive meals. Just to name a few.

Sign-up at:

www.encorebookclub.com

View a complete list of our

Best Selling Recipe Book Series:

www.encorebookclub.com/booklist

Thank You For Your Purchase!

We know you have many choices when it comes to ready and recipe books. Your patronage is sincerely appreciated. If you would like to provide us direct feedback, go to www.encorebookclub.com/feedback.

Consider Writing an Amazon Review!

Happy with this book? If so, writing a positive review is greatly appreciated. It helps others know it's a quality book and allows us to continue to promote our positive message. Cheers!

Made in the USA
Middletown, DE
06 December 2016